The Ultimate Guide for Finding and Winning More Money for College Now

ASHLEY HILL

ISBN: 0692657126
ISBN-13: 978-0692657126

DEDICATION

I dedicate this book to every student around the world who desires to find and win more scholarships for college now. You don't need a secret tip or special formula because you already have what you need to create strong scholarship applications to increase your chances of winning scholarship dollars. You are unique, talented, and your life experiences can't be imitated by anyone else. Scholarship judges want to see your unique qualities, talents, and achievements throughout your scholarship applications. I am going to teach you how to use your talents and achievements to find and win more scholarship dollars throughout this book.

CONTENTS

ACKNOWLEDGMENTS

First, I thank God for giving me the insight and strategies to help students and families learn how to use talents and achievements to find and win scholarships. I thank my parents for their love, prayers, and guidance. Thanks, Mom and Dad, for the sacrifices you made during my college preparation journey to help me find and win scholarships. I thank my brothers and family for their support and encouragement. I thank my team for helping me to share scholarship search and application strategies with students and families around the world. I believe that no one is successful alone. Thank you for the long talks, suggestions, and your consistent diligence in helping me to fulfill my purpose to serve others.

CHAPTER 1

WELCOME TO THE WORLD OF SCHOLARSHIPS

"The competition in the world of scholarships becomes irrelevant when you focus on your talents and achievements". — Ashley Hill

Introduction

The purpose of this guide is to give you all of the information that you need to find the scholarships that fit you and detailed information to increase your chances of winning scholarship dollars. By the end of this book, you will know exactly what you need to do to start finding more money for college today.

There are three core beliefs that you must understand about the world of scholarships to truly be able to find and win more scholarships. These three core beliefs are

1. **There is no scholarship season because scholarship opportunities are available all year long.**

2. **The competition surrounding scholarships becomes irrelevant when students focus on their unique qualities, talents, and achievements.**

3. **Merit scholarship (not based on income) opportunities levels the playing field which gives all students the chance to find and win more money for college.**

I want you to read these core beliefs until you can say them from memory. Why? These beliefs are a part of the mindset of scholarship winners. You need to develop the right mindset to win scholarships.

My Story

I believe that it is important to share my scholarship search and application journey with you to encourage and show you that you can lower the costs of your college education with merit scholarships. My college preparation journey began at a very young age (9 years old). My parents made sure that I was very active in my community with volunteer organizations. They took me on informal campus visits to the local colleges. They helped me to get early exposure to career fields that interested me including STEM careers. I attended my first college fair at 13 years old which eventually led to meeting college admissions representatives from my best-fit college, Kent State University. Ultimately, I decided to attend Kent State University after attending the local college fair several years in a row. I contributed my successful college preparation to my parents who created an environment for me to thrive in college and beyond.

Honestly, I wasn't worried about getting into college because I had prepared for many years. However, I was unsure of how my family and I were going to pay for college. I knew I was going to college and I was willing to put in the work to get scholarships to keep the costs of my college education as low as possible. Fortunately, my parents made sure that I was active in the community from an early age. I had a large amount of volunteer hours which increased my chances of receiving scholarships. Also, my parents showed me how to connect with the right people such as mentors and people working successfully in my desired career field. They put the right people around me who would later go on to write letters of recommendation for scholarship applications, recommend me for internships, and nominate me for awards. I wasn't aware at the time, but I had built a team of scholarship resources around me. With this information, I began to help younger kids in my neighborhood. I had no idea at that time that helping the other students would have a great impact on my career and life today.

Even though I took the initiative to search and apply for scholarships, my parents checked in with me regularly to get updates on my progress throughout the scholarship application process. As I started to receive notifications that I had won a scholarship, I was encouraged to continue to applying for even more scholarships. I treated searching for scholarships like a job. By the time that I graduated from high school, the majority of my college tuition was covered with scholarships.

I was even more at ease knowing that I didn't have to take out a huge loan to cover my college education. In addition to the scholarships, I began my college career at Kent State University with college credits which helped me to reduce the cost of my education. I participated in the Ohio PSEO program (Post-Secondary Enrollment Options) which allowed me to start as second-semester freshman at Kent State University because I attended a local college as a high school senior for free. Also, I applied for an early college program with Kent State University that allowed me to receive college credits and mentorship opportunities during the summer session prior to my first year at Kent State University at no cost to me.

Even in my freshman year of college, I won a $10,000 scholarship as a part of my internship program to help me get early career exposure in research and presenting research topics before faculty, classmates, and staff. I had no knowledge about the internship opportunity until my graduate assistant instructor in one of my biology lab courses encouraged me to apply for the program. I had taken the time to develop a relationship with her outside of the classroom and she kindly gave me insight into the application process. The day of the interview, I walk into the room and look at the committee of judges. Guess who was sitting on the committee? My graduate assistant instructor! She smiled. I said a quick prayer and answered all of the committee's questions. I received notification a few weeks later that I was accepted into the program. I used a portion of those funds to take summer courses for the duration of my college career at Kent State University and was able to graduate in three years.

In the midst of a successful year, I didn't realize that I was getting ready to face a challenge that is a major reason behind why I am passionate about helping you find and win your best fit scholarships today. During winter break before sophomore year, I received a notice from the financial aid office that I needed to pay my remaining tuition balance for sophomore year due to the fact that I had non-renewable scholarships. Non-renewable scholarships are funds that you receive one time. Initially, I wanted to panic because my remaining 3 years at Kent State University would have been covered if all of my scholarships were renewable. I knew that I needed to stay calm and seek a resolution for this issue. I knew that my parents didn't want to take on another loan, so that wasn't an option. The uncertainty of how to cover the remaining tuition balance bothered me. I prayed about what to do and decided to call the financial aid director. I had developed a relationship with her since meeting with her on a campus visit during my junior year of high school. She remembered me and was very helpful. She offered to review my financial aid package as well as informed me of scholarship opportunities and even emergency funding offered by Kent State University. I applied for those scholarships and waited to hear from the financial aid office. While I was waiting for the outcome of applying for the scholarships, I prepared a letter to appeal my financial aid package in the event that I needed to mail it to the financial aid office (I will share more about the financial aid appeal letter in Chapter 8). As each day inched closer to the deadline, I remained patient, prayerful, and focused on my ultimate goal of graduating from college. With three days before the tuition balance was due, I received a call from the financial aid office. The lady simply said, "Ms. Hill, I see that you had a previous tuition balance, but the tuition balance has been covered. We will see you on campus next week". I didn't ask any questions. I thanked her and hung up the phone. I began to thank God that I was able to return to college. I finished that semester, graduated from Kent State University, and obtained research positions at major corporations after college graduation. Yet, I never forgot that experience nor the feelings of uncertainty. So, I decided to take my research and networking skills plus behind-the-scenes knowledge from scholarship judges in addition to my own scholarship search and application process to help you.

The biggest message that I want you to take away from this book is that you can find and win scholarship with a proven step-by-step simple solution starting today! You already qualify for merit scholarships. It is time for you to match your qualifications with the merit scholarships that are looking for students like you!

Don't Believe These Scholarship Myths!

Before I discuss how you can find and win more money for college, I want to debunk the common myths surrounding searching and applying for scholarships. I strongly believe that you must begin this process with the right mindset to become scholarship winners.

I can wait until a year before I start college.

This statement makes the assumption that a student will win some or all of the scholarships that he or she applies for during the year before starting college. This is a dangerous assumption because there is no guarantee that one will win one, some, or all scholarships. Also, delaying this process means that a student misses the scholarship opportunities that are available every day. You don't want to leave any scholarship dollars on the table. Start as early as possible.

I don't qualify for a lot of scholarships.

How do you know that you don't qualify for many scholarships? This thought indicates that you may not understand the world of scholarships. In the world of scholarships, you absolutely qualify for merit scholarships. Merit scholarships are based on your talents and achievements. You will discover in Chapter 2 how to take all of your experiences, talents, and achievements and increase your chances of winning scholarships.

I don't have time to search for scholarships.

Is it a fact that you don't have time or is it a fact that you haven't made searching for a scholarship a priority in your life? The truth is that you do have the time to search for scholarships. You may not have as much as time as the next person, but you have to focus on how to maximize your time to search for scholarships. The best way to maximize your time when searching for scholarships is to get organized and create a strategy so you know exactly where and how to search for scholarships.

I am undecided on a college or college major and probably won't qualify for a lot of scholarships.

This statement indicates that you may not understand the world of scholarships. You don't have to select your college or college major for many of the merit scholarship opportunities. Merit scholarships focus on talents and achievements. If you find merit scholarship opportunities that fit you that require you to select a college or college major, reserve these scholarships until you have made your selections. But, don't let this minor detail stop you from searching for scholarships now.

There are too many scholarships for me. I feel overwhelmed and haven't applied to any of them.

Yes, there are millions of dollars in scholarship opportunities available to students. Searching through thousands of these scholarship opportunities can certainly make you feel overwhelmed if you don't have a method to cut out the scholarships that don't fit you. Every scholarship isn't designed to fit you. You have to focus on your talents and achievements when searching for your best fit scholarships. Having a narrow focus will decrease the number of scholarships you have to review, saves time, and makes you feel less stressful about this process.

There are only scholarships available at certain times a year.

You have to go back to the core beliefs that I mentioned at the beginning of this chapter. There is no scholarship season. In other words, there is no specific time of the year that scholarships are only available. Now, each organization has the right to choose the period of time that it will receive scholarships and select a winner. However, all organizations do not select the same time period. Literally, there are scholarship opportunities available almost every day of the year. This is why you must continually search for scholarships from elementary school to graduate school. Yes, there are scholarships for students as young as five years old (through the Doodle 4 Google program) to doctoral students completing their graduate studies.

Set your Scholarship Search and Application Goal by Having the "Money Talk"

Now that you have the right foundation of information about scholarships, it is time to discuss setting your goals to make applying for scholarships simple and as less stressful as possible. I highly encourage you to complete this task before you start searching for scholarships.

1. Determine how you will pay for college (scholarships, grants, employment, loans, or a combination of financial sources).

Special Note (Parents): First, I want you to sit down with your child and discuss how to pay for your child's college education. I call this the "Money Talk". You need to have a very honest and open discussion with your child and let him or her know if you are contributing to paying for college and an estimated amount. Also, you will need to let your child know if you will require him or her to contribute to paying for college (working and/or applying for scholarships). If other family members or friends will contribute to your child's college education, they need to be a part of the "Money Talk" as well.

2. Visit your future or current college's website to get an estimate of the total costs of your college education. Don't forget to include costs such as books, cell phone, car insurance, or membership fees. Feel free to use cost calculators as well.

Special Note (Parents): The "Money Talk" is most effective when you and your child have an estimate of the total costs of college (beyond tuition and room and board). You can go to the financial aid website of your child's desired college or search for college cost calculators in your favorite search engine if your child is undecided or too young to apply for college.

3. Based on the estimated total costs of your college education, determine how much funding you will need in scholarships to help pay for your education.

Special Note (Parents): Once you have the total estimated amount, you will subtract the amount that you will contribute to paying for your college.

The remaining amount will determine an estimate of how many scholarships for your child needs to cover the cost. If your child needs $10,000+, he or she will need a more aggressive plan of action as compared to if your child needs $2,000 for college. Whether you are paying for your child's entire college education or contributing half of the amount, I want to challenge you to require your child to contribute to paying for his or her college education by applying for scholarships. *Why pay for college with your money when your child can win scholarships based on his or her achievements?* I have seen too many families frustrated due to the lack of discussing how to pay for college during the child's senior year of high school. This is too late.

4. If your financial situation changes or if you decide to pursue a different college, you can make adjustments to the estimated costs to determine your goal for the scholarship amount that you will need to pay for your education.

Special Note (Parents): Please note that the "Money Talk" isn't a one-time event. This should be a regular discussion as your child gets closer to applying for college. Paying for college is a team event and everyone has a role in this process.

Next, I am going to discuss the other aspects in the world of scholarships that you need to keep in mind as you search for scholarships. There is no question that you have a busy schedule. If you invest the time to create a schedule to manage the scholarship search and application process, you will be able to maximize the time you set aside to find scholarship dollars.

How many hours should I spend searching for scholarships?

The truth is that no two students nor their circumstances are alike. I advise you to spend a minimum of 3 – 5 hours searching and applying for scholarships weekly. If you start early and consistently, you can decrease the amount of hours to 2 -3 hours weekly. The key is to create a schedule that fits your life. Time is a constant which means that everyone receives the same 24 hours every day. Scholarship searching is not time management, but priority management. You must make searching and applying for scholarships a priority in your life.

Special Note (Parents): I advise students to spend a minimum of 3-5 hours searching and applying for scholarships weekly during the school year and 15-20 hours weekly during extended school breaks. If your child is heavily involved in activities outside of the classroom, I advise you to encourage your child to spend the majority of his or her time searching and applying for scholarships on the weekends. If your child has a lighter schedule, I advise you to encourage your child to divide their time searching and applying for scholarships between weekdays and weekends. For school breaks, your child should treat scholarship searching like a job. If they spend 2 hours and win $500, he or she earned $250 an hour. That's more than most full time employees!

Organizing the scholarship search process and scholarship applications

The scholarship search and application process can become overwhelming quickly if you don't have an organization system. Let's talk about ways that you can get organized in the scholarship search process. Remember that you have to make an organization system that fits your needs.

Special Note (Parents): With a clear goal in mind, it is time for your child to organize how he or she will maintain a scholarships list, scholarship applications, and requirements including scholarship application deadlines. As I mentioned earlier in this chapter, paying for college is a team sport. It even takes a team to search and apply for scholarships. Your role in your child's team is to support, provide guidance, serve as a resource, and present scholarship opportunities to your child. I am going to discuss the other members of your child's scholarship strategy team in Chapter 2.

1. Create online and/or get physical folders to organize current scholarship applications, completed scholarship applications, scholarship essays, scholarship website lists.

Special Note (Parents): I suggest that you work with your child to combine online and offline tools to organize the scholarship search and application process. During my scholarship journey, I created a folder named Scholarships which contained several folders including "Scholarships (Current Year)", "Scholarship Applications Process", "Scholarship Applications Completed", "Scholarship Essays", and "Scholarship Websites" on my computer. As I searched for scholarships or worked on scholarship applications, I placed the scholarship websites, scholarship applications, and scholarship essays in the appropriate folders.

2. I highly recommend that you use Google Calendar and schedule deadlines with reminders at least two weeks prior to the deadline.

Special Note (Parent): You can have your child to add your email address to the Google Calendar to get alerts to help remind your child to complete scholarship applications.

What about scholarship scams?

Unfortunately, there are organizations that are behind scholarship scams. So, I caution you to be aware of scholarship scams. The signs of scholarship scams include organizations that require you to pay a fee to apply for scholarships, require you to provide your social security number on the scholarship application, and have negative press regarding suspected or confirmed fraudulent activity. If you feel that a scholarship opportunity is possibly a scam, feel free to research and ask others.

Take action!

I want you to schedule time as soon as possible to create your scholarship goal and a system to help you stay organized and manage your priority properly.

CHAPTER 2

YOUR ROAD MAP TO SCHOLARSHIP DOLLARS: SCHOLARSHIP RÉSUMÉ

"Creating your scholarship résumé is one of the most important tasks that you can do to show you exactly which scholarships will fit you and where to go find them".
— Ashley Hill

Introduction

A scholarship résumé is a listing of your personal data including your talents, achievements, and leadership experience. In other words, your scholarship résumé is you on paper. Your scholarship résumé is so crucial in helping you find the right scholarships that fit you that I am spending this entire chapter on teaching you how to create your scholarship résumé!

Before you search for one scholarship, you must create your scholarship résumé!

Whether you are a future college student, homeschool students, current college student, adult student, transfer student, international student, or graduate student, you need a clear path from where you are today to your scholarship dollars. One of the greatest mistakes that I see students making when searching for scholarships is not taking the time to create a roadmap to scholarships that fit them. Lack of direction creates many issues including frustration and feeling overwhelmed with trying to figure out where are the best fit scholarships. Even worse, I have talked to students who would rather give up their search for scholarships because they are tired of following leads to scholarship opportunities that don't fit them. Let's end the frustration and stress surrounding where to find scholarship opportunities.

Why do I need to create a scholarship résumé?

In one word, clarity! There is so much confusion in the scholarship search and application process for reasons including the fact that a wealth of information that doesn't necessarily apply to each student. What's the solution to resolving confusion? Clarity. It is time to get crystal clear about how and where to find your scholarships. Your scholarship résumé is going to reveal to you the key information that you will use to focus in on the best fit scholarship opportunities for you. The cool part about your scholarship résumé is that each section and sub-section represents the type of scholarship opportunities available to you!

What are the other benefits of creating my scholarship résumé?

You will be able to use your scholarship résumé in the following ways:

Creating strong scholarship essays. You will learn in Chapter 6 that the key to a strong scholarship essay is answering the question or prompt with emphasis on your leadership skills and experience. How will you know what experiences to share in your essay? You will refer to your scholarship résumé to select your leadership experiences that align with the particular scholarship essay requirements.

Creating attractive scholarship applications. In order to create attractive scholarship applications, you need to present the best representation of you to the scholarship judges. What is the best representation of you? The answer is in the information you will list in your scholarship résumé. Remember that your scholarship résumé is a snapshot of you and your experiences which you must share with scholarship judges on your scholarship applications. Instead of wondering what to share with them, you will simply select your experiences that fit in with the scope of the scholarship application.

How to Create your Scholarship Résumé

We are going to walk through how to create your scholarship résumé step by step. I want to warn you that you will need to invest time to create your scholarship résumé, but the benefit of knowing exactly where to find your best fit scholarships is worth the investment of your time! Get your pen and paper, iPad, tablet, or feel free to use your laptop/desktop computer. Your scholarship résumé is going to be organized into the following sections:

Personal
Family
Academic
Volunteer/Leadership/Work Experience
Career

Organizing your scholarship résumé into these sections will make it easier for you to reference your information when searching for your scholarships later. Let's discuss each section and the type of information you should list under each section. Make sure to complete each section with all related details – big or small. What you consider to be a small detail could be a major detail in the eyes of your scholarship judges.

Personal Section

What should I include in the personal section?

The personal section of your scholarship résumé will include your gender, residence (city and state), ethnicity, height, health challenges (mental or physical), military affiliations (you, your parents, and//or grandparents), religious affiliations, skills, special talents, passions (environmental, politics, working with youth, etc.), travel experiences, and hobbies.

Why is this information to include in my scholarship résumé?

There are organizations seeking to give scholarships to students based on gender, residence, ethnicity, and all of the other items in your personal section. You don't want to leave any scholarship dollars on the table. If an item doesn't apply to you, feel free to skip to the next item on the list that does apply to you. So, you need to first be aware of all scholarship opportunities that fit you so you can apply for them! One of the most common statements that students tell me is they didn't know there were certain scholarships to fit them. My goal in this book is to expose you to all of the scholarship opportunities around you. The best way that I can help you is by education you on the type of scholarship opportunities available to you.

Special Notes:

1. If you don't feel comfortable discussing health challenges, I want you to understand that you are not required to share them on your scholarship applications. If you are comfortable with sharing your health challenges, I am going to share strategies for discussing

health challenges generally in Chapter 6 and 7.

2. For military affiliations, please include those who are currently serving as well as those who are military veterans.

3. For skills and special talents, don't be afraid to ask your friends and family to give insight into your skills and talents. Sometimes, you may be talented in an area that you don't think is a big deal because it comes naturally to you. Also, I encourage you ask your scholarship resource team. I will discuss this more in Chapter 3.

4. For travel experience, don't forget to include international travel as well as your out of state travel experiences. Yes, there are scholarship opportunities for students who have travelled to certain places. No place is too big or too small. Also, write down notes about your purpose for visiting those places. This could be very helpful for your scholarship essays and applications.

Let's move on to the family section of your scholarship résumé.

Family Section

What should I include in the family section?

The family section is all about your parent' current position and memberships plus your grandparents' current position and memberships. If your parents or grandparents are retired, please list their former employer in this section. For memberships, don't forget to include sororities, fraternities, industry groups, and even religious memberships if they apply to your family. Lastly, write down anyone in your family (or family friends) who are members of organizations that would interest you.

Why is this important for me to include in my scholarship résumé?

There are many employers that offer scholarship dollars to children and grandchildren of employees including retired employees. Likewise, many membership organizations provide scholarship opportunities to children or grandchildren of members. This could equal thousands of dollars going towards your college education. Lastly, I encourage you to write down anyone in your family or even family friends who are working in careers that match your career interests. They could be a potential member of your scholarship resource team and could be a source of scholarships specific to your career.

Next, let's discuss the academic section of your scholarship résumé.

Academic Section

What should I include in my academic section?

This section is all about your academic skills and activities that you do connected with your school. In this section, you will include your current GPA, academic awards, after school activities, sports activities, and sports awards. Please keep in mind that no academic award is too small. For sports if you won player of the week or your statistics were listed in the local newspaper or mentioned on the news (check their website for a link to the story mentioning you), write it down in this section. Even though I focus on merit scholarships which aren't based on academics or income level, you should still challenge yourself to do well in your classes.

Bonus Tip: If you have won scholarships or contests in the past, make sure to include this information on your scholarship applications. Why? You're smart, talented, and wonderful, but it is always best to allow others to brag on you.

Volunteer/Leadership/Work Experience Section

Let's keep going and talk about the volunteer/leadership/work experience section. In this section, you will include summer programs or camps (for any purpose), volunteer activities, memberships, leadership activities, leadership awards, internships and work experience.

Volunteer experience (unpaid work) is crucial to your success in winning scholarship dollars. The key for completing this section is to include the organization, specific details of your activities or tasks, memorable moments, and contact information. The time to gather all of this information is not when you're completing your scholarship application.

I want you to understand the fact that you are a leader. You don't have to be a CEO, president, or have any title in a group to be considered a leader. I want you to keep this simple definition of a leaders in mind – influence. A leader is influential. I can promise you that you have leadership experience. Let's go over a few examples:

Are you a member of a group and you led a project?
Do you own a business (including seasonal businesses)?
Have you ever started a fundraiser for a charity?
Have you ever noticed a better way to complete a task in your work?

Guess what? Leaders are involved in the type of activities that I have just mentioned above. You are a leader.

Career Section

The last section of your scholarship résumé is the career section. In this section, you will include your desired career and major. This is the shortest section of your scholarship résumé but it is very powerful. The key to completing this section is focusing on the skills that you will need to be successful in your desired career. This is especially helpful when you are unsure of your future career. You don't need to know your future career of college to be eligible for scholarships. I want to spend time exploring areas that interest you such as Math, English, Foreign Language, and Education and brainstorm what you imagine yourself doing in those areas.

Special Note (Undergraduate, Adult, and Graduate Students): I want you to be aware that many of your scholarship opportunities will be based on your future or current career field. I encourage you to write notes in this section of your scholarship résumé about your career interests with specific details such as you want to pursue nursing with pediatric patients.

CHAPTER 3

CREATING YOUR SCHOLARSHIP STRATEGY: SCHOLARSHIP RÉSUMÉ + SCHOLARSHIP STRATEGY TEAM

"Your scholarship strategy is the GPS that you will need to use to follow your roadmap (scholarship résumé) on your journey to finding and winning scholarships that best fit you". – Ashley Hill

Introduction

What is a scholarship search strategy?

A scholarship strategy is a plan that shows what scholarships will fit you and the information from your scholarship résumé that you should include in your scholarship application to increase your chances of winning those scholarship dollars. Your scholarship strategy will help you to gain clarity on how and where to search using the details from your scholarship résumé. Please note that every item on your scholarship résumé will not be applicable to every scholarship application that you complete. You have to strategically select details from your experiences, talents, and achievements that will enhance your scholarship application. A scholarship strategy is not complete without a scholarship strategy team. I am going to discuss scholarship strategy teams in a later section in this chapter. For now, I want you to remember the formula for a scholarship strategy which is your scholarship résumé plus your scholarship strategy team.

Who needs to create a scholarship strategy?

If you are in grades K-12 (public, private or homeschool), you need a scholarship strategy. If you are currently attending college as an undergraduate or graduate student, you need a scholarship strategy. If you are a future or current international student, you need a scholarship strategy. If you need scholarships to complete a few college courses to get a certification to get a promotion at work or transition to a new career, you need a scholarship strategy. I hope I have made it clear that you need a scholarship strategy! I am going to show you step-by-step how to create your scholarship strategy with specific advice for K-12 students, current college students (undergraduate and graduate), adult students, and international students.

When should I create my scholarship strategy?

You will need to create your scholarship résumé before you start searching for scholarships. Make sure that your scholarship résumé is complete as possible because you will need to select details from your scholarship résumé to create your scholarship strategy. I strongly advise you not to start searching for scholarships until you have created your scholarship résumé. Why? As I mentioned in Chapter 2, one of the frustrations with searching for scholarships is students don't know where to find scholarships that fit them. The solution is to create a scholarship strategy so you can use your time wisely.

Why do I need to create a scholarship strategy to help me find scholarships?

As I mentioned in the first statement of this chapter, you have to think of your scholarship strategy like a GPS giving you directions to your destination. Yes, your scholarship résumé tells you what scholarships fit you, but that is only one part of what you need to create winning scholarship applications. You need to know how to actually make your scholarship applications command the attention of scholarship judges. You discover how to make strong scholarship applications in the process of creating your scholarship applications.

Now, let's discuss all of the parts of your scholarship strategy. The first part of your scholarship strategy is your scholarship résumé and the second part is your scholarship resource team. We have already discussed you're your scholarship résumé contains all of your data which includes your talents, achievements, leadership experiences, hobbies, and future career interests.

Next, review each section of your scholarship résumé and write synonyms for each item that you listed in your scholarship résumé. The reason you're going to create this list is because those synonyms will become your search terms that you are going to use to search for local, national, and international scholarship opportunities. At the end of this exercise, you will actually have a list of all of the ways that you need to search in your local community as well as for national and international scholarships.

Why do I need to create synonyms?

Synonyms are very important because they help you to expand your scholarship search efforts beyond the information you listed in your scholarship résumé. Organizations that provide scholarship opportunities do not use the same words in their scholarship information and requirements. One company may provide scholarships for students pursuing a career in government while another company may provide scholarships for students pursuing a career in cybersecurity. Since you don't know ahead of time of the wording that the organizations will use, it is best to create a list with as many synonyms as possible.

Personal Section

Let's start with the first section of your scholarship résumé which is your personal section. You should have listed your personal information including gender, residence, and any health challenges. So, take each item that you listed in this section and write down other words to describe your personal information. For example, you may have listed that you live in Elmhurst, Illinois. Another way to describe your city would be to list your county and other major cities near Elmhurst such as Chicago, Illinois. Now you will be able to search for scholarships in Elmhurst, Chicago, Illinois, your county, and major cities near Elmhurst. This is crucial to have several search terms to use when you are searching for local scholarship opportunities. I will give you specific local scholarship sources and strategies in the next chapter.

Family Section

The next section in your scholarship résumé is the family section which includes your parents' employment history and their memberships. I discussed in the previous chapter that you should include your parents' current employer, former employer (due to retirement), and any associations or memberships. Don't forget to include your grandparents as well. Let's say that your parents work in the medical industry. In this section of your scholarship résumé, you will list synonyms such as specific position (nursing, for example) and other words to describe the medical field such as medicine, health sciences, preventative care, and health care. Please do the same exercise for memberships and associations. So, if your parents work in the nursing field, they most likely are associated with nursing groups, professional associations, medical group, or health association. If your parents are retired, you will need to create a list of synonyms for that career field as well. For example, if your parents retired from the finance industry, your list of synonyms should include the specific company name, finance, business, financial services, business, and financial planning. Ultimately, you want to have a list of all of the different search terms to help you find all available scholarships that fit you. This is how you know exactly what you're looking for when searching for scholarships.

Academic Section

Next, let's discuss the next section of your scholarship résumé which is your academic section. This section includes your academic skills, activities, academic awards, after school activities, sports activities, and sports awards. For this section, you need to brainstorm other words you can use to describe your academic information, activities, and sports. If you are in college and play lacrosse, you may want to include collegiate sports or outdoor sports to this section. If you won any academic awards, you may want to list the subject of the award (such as Math) or the purpose of the award (such as 4.0 GPA).

Leadership and Volunteer Experiences Section

The next section in your scholarship résumé focuses on leadership and volunteer experiences. In this section, I want you to think about the type of experience that you gained as well as the purpose of the experience when selecting synonyms for how you will search for scholarships later. For example, if you served as a volunteer abroad with an organization that works with youth, three words should stand out to you. Those three words are volunteer, abroad, and youth. So, your list of synonyms will include volunteer overseas, volunteer abroad, volunteer with youth, and missions. At this point, you should include specific activities that you did with the volunteer organization. Did you lead an activity with the kids? What were your responsibilities during your time abroad? Where did you travel to volunteer with the youth? These questions will ultimately lead you to be able to add more synonyms to your scholarship résumé. Why are these questions important? Your search terms that you pull from your answers to these questions can lead to scholarship dollars. If you found a scholarship organization looking for students with volunteer experience working with youth. Do you qualify? Yes!

Work Experience Section

Lastly, I want to discuss work experience and how this can help you to qualify for more scholarships. Whether you work all year long or seasonally in your own business or for an employer, I want you to think about your industry and your work responsibilities. If you started your own business, you are certainly a leader. Think about your type of business, who you serve in your business, and your accomplishments in your business. For example, if you own a landscaping business, your synonyms may include small business, entrepreneur, business serving residential clients, or landscaping. If you work for a company, I want you think about your work duties, projects, and accomplishments. If you work on a team, focus on your contributions to the team. Perhaps you improved a process or organized project update meetings which would qualify you for scholarships that focus on leadership. You don't have to be the manager or project leader to be a leader. I will discuss this in more detail later in this chapter.

Career Section

The last section of your scholarship résumé is the career section. If you are pursuing a specific career field or are looking for scholarships to advance in your career, you should have included this in your scholarship résumé from the previous chapter. As I have discussed with the previous sections of your scholarship résumé, you need to brainstorm a list of synonyms for the career section that you can add to your search terms to find the scholarships that fit you. For example, if your future or current career is economics or finance, you should brainstorm a list of synonyms such as business, financial services, and math. As with the other sections of your résumé, these synonyms will become the search terms you use to find the scholarships that fit you.

How to Find More Scholarships that Fit You Using Your Scholarship Résumé

So far, we have discussed your scholarship strategy and how to create a list of synonyms from your scholarship résumé that you will use as search terms when searching for scholarships. Now, I am going to discuss ways that you can find more scholarships using the information that you already have on your scholarship résumé. In my experience, I have seen many scholarship résumés with little to no volunteer and leadership experience. This is a major issue because scholarship judges want to see evidence of your leadership skills. I want you to review your scholarship résumé and identify areas where you can get more experience or get involved in more activities. I can promise you that if you make the time to gain more leadership and volunteer experience, you will increase your eligibility for more scholarships. Also, I encourage you to pursue more activities that align with your talents and achievements. Focus on improving your academic skills as well. For example, if you are an adult student, I highly encourage you to gain leadership experience through your current position as well as find opportunities to volunteer with a local organization. If you are a future college student, select several after school activity clubs to join and focus on gaining leadership experience. When you create your scholarship résumé as early as possible, you have time to fill in any gaps in your scholarship résumé and get more experience which increases your chances of winning scholarship dollars.

How to Use Your Leadership to Find More Scholarships

I want to discuss leadership and the true definition of leadership in this next section because this is the top item that scholarship judges want to see in your scholarship applications. This is actually a two-step process to using your leadership abilities to help you find and win scholarships. First, you need to gain leadership experience. Secondly, you must communicate your leadership abilities to the scholarship judges in a way that increases your chances of winning scholarship dollars. Leadership has to be tied into the overall theme of your scholarship applications.

What is leadership?

I define leadership simply as influence. A leader has influence within a group of people to accomplish a common goal. How do you define leadership? A leader is not necessarily the CEO, president, or manager, but you can lead within your group. You can lead a project within one of your groups or launch your own project. Additionally, leaders overcome challenges, effectively solve problems, take risks, and communicate effectively. By the way, these are all qualities that you should display on your scholarship applications.

How to Leverage your Leadership Skills on Your Scholarship Applications

Before you can leverage your leadership skills on your scholarship applications, you need to spend time gaining leadership experience. Leadership skill development opportunities can be divided into joining groups that are already established or launching a new group or project.

You can gain leadership skills in your current position or by starting your own business. You can join after school activity groups or partner with volunteer organizations and join the planning committees. There are literally leadership opportunities all around you. You have to recognize them and take advantage of them. Now, I am going to discuss the four main areas that you can use to leverage your leadership skills to strengthen your scholarship applications and increase your chances of winning scholarship dollars. Also, I will share ways that you can effectively communicate your leadership experience to scholarship judges.

1. **Gain Leadership Experience through Volunteer Experience.** Volunteer experience allows you to work with an organization and help lead a project, plan an event, or manage a fundraiser to bring about change in the lives of those in the community. As you seek volunteer opportunities, seek ways to lead within the organization. Don't hesitate to ask how you can contribute to the volunteer organization and lead in that area. If you desire to launch your own project, think about how you can influence your community for the good. Your project can be very simple and on your street or it can be more complex and involve your entire neighborhood. Make sure that you are documenting your volunteer project. You can communicate your volunteer experience directly on your scholarship applications. Make sure that you make the connection between the organization's mission and purpose to your leadership experience through your volunteer experience.

2. **Gain Leadership Experience through Extracurricular Activities.** Whether you are a K-12, undergraduate, graduate, or Adult student, you can use extracurricular activities based on areas including academics, sports, sororities/fraternities, religion, passions, hobbies, and career interests. I encourage you to make time to include these activities into your schedule. If you are unavailable during the week, you can reserve several weekend days to get involved in extracurricular activities. Also, pursue extracurricular activities that interest you. There is no need to choose activities to impress the scholarship judges. Be authentic. You can lead the workouts for your sports team, lead a project within the academic club, or plan industry events in the area of your career interests with the planning committee. When you prepare your scholarship applications, focus on communicating specific skills with examples to show your leadership experience through extracurricular activities. For example, if you are leading workouts with your soccer teammates, you can focus on how you believe in

taking initiative to influence change (healthier team and reduces risk of injury) on your soccer team. This is a great way to show the scholarship judges that you are not only just playing soccer, but you are making positive contributions to the team.

3. **Gain Leadership Experience through Work/Business.** Using your current position or business is a great way to develop leadership experience because you are surrounded by leadership opportunities. Is there a process in your department at work that is broken in some way? Perhaps you can make suggestions to improve the process especially if this will make your job easier to perform. If you have a business, you are leading projects and providing value to your clients daily. I want you to understand from these examples that you don't have to be a manager in your position to be a leader. In fact, you don't have to wait to start influencing change in your place of employment or in your business. You will communicate your skills with specific examples that shows your leadership experience through your work or business on your scholarship applications. Due to the fact that the scholarship judges don't know all of the details of your position or business, you will have to provide specific examples with the leadership skills that you wish to highlight on the scholarship application.

4. **Gain Leadership Experience through Social Media.** One of the signs of a successful leader is a constant state of leadership development. You should always seek opportunities to further develop your leadership abilities. In this day, leadership is on a local, national, and international level. Therefore, you should see opportunities to develop your leadership skills on all levels. In addition to joining extracurricular activities and gaining leadership experience through your work or business, you have the opportunity to influence the world through your thoughts and ideas. Social media is a great way to communicate your passion for protecting the environment, working with the youth, cancer drug research, or even educating others on your current or future career field. How? You can take one or two of your favorite social media platforms such as Twitter or LinkedIn or Facebook and share your skills, talents, and passions with the world. For example, if you are into the arts, you should focus on YouTube and Instagram. If you are interested in politics and desire to pursue a law degree, you should share content on LinkedIn, a social media platform for professionals. I can tell you that you can influence the world for

good. You will be amazed at the opportunities and relationships that come from sharing your content on a local, national, and international levels. Now, when you are completing your scholarship applications, make sure to incorporate your content with how you have learned and progressed as a global leader. I guarantee this will get the attention of the scholarship judges.

Your Scholarship Strategy Team

Even though your scholarship application process is about you, it truly takes a village to find and win scholarships. I like to call this village your scholarship strategy team. In this section, I am going to discuss why you need a scholarship strategy team and how your scholarship strategy team can help you increase your chances of winning more scholarship dollars.

What is a scholarship strategy team?

A scholarship strategy team is a group of people who can assist you with the entire scholarship application process including guiding you to scholarship resources, helping you to review your scholarship essay, prepare for interviews (if necessary), and help you strengthen your scholarship applications.

Why do I need to create a scholarship strategy team?

You need to create a scholarship strategy team because you only have your personal network and your knowledge of scholarship resources. You get the opportunity to take advantage of a much larger network of people and resources when you are able to tap into the resources of others. Also, you may discover that you have a challenge with writing strong scholarship essays. With a scholarship strategy team, you can have strong writers and editors on your team to make sure that your scholarship essays are strong. The scholarship search and application process becomes more manageable for you when you have a team of people around you to help you create winning scholarship applications.

Who should be a member of my scholarship strategy team?

Your scholarship strategy team should include your family, school counselors, financial aid staff, college admissions staff, educators, people who work in your desired career field, and people with strong writing or editing skills.

How can I find people to be a part of my scholarship strategy team?

Most of the people on your scholarship strategy team will be people you know in your community such as educators and school counselors. Start on the local level and then reach out to your future or current college admissions and financial aid staff. Lastly, feel free to reach out to people outside of your state or country if you still need additional assistance.

When should I create a scholarship strategy team?

You need to create your scholarship strategy team as soon as you are ready to start searching for scholarships. Keep in mind that you may start with only three people on your scholarship strategy team, but you can always add other people over team. Please don't wait until you have a full scholarship strategy team to start searching and applying for scholarships.

Special Note (All Students): Please note that your scholarship résumé is not designed to be a one-time activity. As you progress through your college years, you should continue to add volunteer and leadership experiences as well as academic awards to your scholarship résumé. When you continue to develop yourself and add your experiences to your scholarship résumé, you open the doors for future scholarship opportunities. I recommend that you revisit your scholarship résumé quarterly to add experiences.

Take action!

Review your scholarship résumé and make sure that you have synonyms listed for each section of your scholarship résumé. Make a list of at least three ways that you can gain more leadership experience.

CHAPTER 4

LOCAL SCHOLARSHIP SEARCH STRATEGIES

"The first place that you need to search for scholarships is in your local community because you already qualify for them. Start there!" – Ashley Hill

Introduction

When you start searching for scholarships at the local level, you automatically increase your chances of winning local scholarships because everyone isn't eligible for these scholarship opportunities. The great news is that local scholarship opportunities are available to students of all ages and academic levels.

What is a local scholarship?

It is very important for you to understand the concept of local scholarships so you can find your best fit scholarships in your community. Typically, students search for local scholarships by focusing in their school district or neighborhood. I want to challenge this definition of local scholarships and encourage you to expand your view of local scholarships to any scholarship opportunity in your neighborhood, city, and state. But, wait, isn't a scholarship on the state level considered a national scholarship? Yes, and no. In general, anything on the state level is considered to be national, but not in the case of scholarships. Local scholarships are scholarships that are local to you including your neighborhood city, county, and state. When you have this perspective, you open the door for more scholarships that fit you.

Special Note (International Students): If you are an international student you will need to focus on foundations and government-sponsored programs in your resident country for local scholarship opportunities. I will discuss this topic in the "Government Websites" section below. Also, I am going to share more ways that you can find scholarships in the next chapter.

Special Note (K-12 (including Homeschool), Undergraduate, Graduate, and Adult Students): As I discuss each scholarship source and strategy below, please understand that the scholarship requirements may not specifically state that the scholarship is intended for high school or graduate students only. If this is the case, you are eligible for those scholarships as long as you meet all of the other requirements. Look for my special notes and bonus tips to help you get the most benefit from these local scholarship sources and strategies.

I am going to give you examples of scholarship search strategies through the rest of this chapter based on the following career strategies:

Health and Medicine
Arts, Media, Entertainment, Sports
STEM (Science, Technology, Engineering, Math)
Social Services (Education, Government)
Business
Social Sciences
Trades (Construction, Culinary, Transportation, Personal Services)

The best way to benefit from the following scholarship sources and strategies is to apply the information to your situation. In fact, I want you to read this chapter with your scholarship résumé. Write notes under each section of your scholarship résumé about scholarship opportunities and contact information for specific groups or organizations providing those scholarships.

Let's get started.

Local Scholarship Sources and Strategies

Your Favorite Search Engine

I want to discuss this source of scholarships and the strategies that you can use right now to find more scholarship dollars because most people start here. As I mentioned in the introduction of this chapter I strongly advise that you begin to search for scholarships on the local level. What I didn't say is that you have to restrict your scholarship search for local scholarships offline. There are local scholarship resources online!

The key to searching for local scholarships in your favorite search engine is pulling information from your scholarship résumé. Why? You don't want to leave any scholarship dollars on the table. While most students may search with phrases such as "scholarships + (insert name of neighborhood)", this will only give you limited search results. I would consider this a first level approach (which works!) but let's dig a little deeper into how to leverage your favorite search engine when searching for local scholarships.

In order to make sure that you find all of the scholarships that will fit you, you need to search for local scholarships that match the information that you have listed on your scholarship résumé. The most important thing that you need to remember is that you must use a combination of your search terms that you created from your scholarship résumé in the previous chapter. For example, you are not just a future student living in Utah. You are a future college student pursuing a career in nursing with over 1,000 hours of community service who is living in Utah. Use all of your search terms.

Bonus Tip: Keep track of expired scholarship opportunities so you can apply for them next year. This will reduce the amount of time searching for scholarships for next year.

School Counselor (K-12 School)

A great resource of scholarships in your community is your school counselor. Typically, school counselors at middle and high schools will have a resource list of scholarship applications for students to apply all year long. I encourage you to visit your school counselor's office regularly (monthly) and ask for scholarship applications. This task accomplishes two purposes You can access scholarships that fit you while building a relationship with your school counselor which will come in handy when you need letters of recommendation and help with your scholarship applications.

Also, many high school counselors will host events during the Fall to help students understand college costs and discuss options for paying for college. I highly encourage you to make plans to attend those events and ask questions.

Additionally, most schools serving K-12 students have a website with information for students, parents, and the community. I strongly advise you to visit your school's website for scholarship opportunities. You will usually find scholarships in the school counseling section of the school's website.

Bonus Tip: Please check for previous scholarship winners that are featured on your school's website. This is not for comparison or to make you feel like you can't win that particular scholarship. I want you to pay attention to the name of the scholarship as well as any information on the scholarship winners. For example, if the organization selected the student because his or her parents serve in the military, this will be great insight into your approach for applying for that scholarship next year. In this example, you have to be careful to understand if having parents in the military is a requirement or if that scholarship winner used his or her parent's military career as an example to strengthen the scholarship application. I will cover this in detail in Chapter 7.

Special Note (K-6 Students): Your scholarship resources will come in the form of traditional scholarship opportunities and contests. For traditional scholarships, I want you to check in with your school counselor at the beginning of the school year and at the end of each school term. Refer to the contest section later in this chapter for specific search techniques.

Special Note (K-12 Homeschool Students): Yes, I know that you don't have a school counselor, however, I am going to show you right now how you can find local scholarships through the school district in your neighborhood. I want you to go to the school district's website and look for the school counseling section for scholarships. You will need to read the requirements very carefully. If you don't see a requirement to be a student at that elementary, middle, or high school, there is a high chance that you are eligible for that particular scholarship.

Other Local K-12 Schools

Do you remember how I discussed earlier in this chapter about expanding your perspective of local scholarships? Let's dig deeper. With the exception of scholarships that are specific to a certain school, you have a good chance of being eligible for scholarships on the websites of all school districts in your city, county, and state (including K-12 homeschool students). I encourage you to search for school districts in your city, county, and state using your favorite search engine. Put all of the names and website links into a document and invest one of your weekends in searching those websites for scholarships.

College (Admissions, Financial Aid, and Specific Department Staff)

If you are a future or current college student attending a local college, I encourage you to take advantage of your future or current college's website for scholarship opportunities. Specifically, I want you to focus on the admissions, financial aid, and department of your future or current degree program areas of the college's website. Many colleges and universities provide an office dedicated to assisting students (including international students) with finding scholarships. If your college provides this opportunity, please take advantage of this resource.

Special Note (Adult and Graduate Students): Scholarships specific to your college or university will be one of the best sources of scholarships to help you complete your college education. I want you to pay special attention to how to put together winning scholarship applications in Chapter 7 so you can make sure you are sending strong scholarship applications to the scholarship committees on campus.

Special Note (International Students): As soon as you choose your college or university, visit the college or university website for scholarships for international students. Also, you can schedule time to speak with the admissions department and office for international students, if available, for scholarships that will fit you. In fact, you may want to target colleges or universities that have large populations of international students. This is a good sign that there could be more scholarships available to you.

Other Local Colleges

This scholarship source is very similar to local scholarships for K-12 school districts. While internal or institutional merit scholarships are for college students attending that specific college, you will find external or private merit scholarships that may fit you in the financial aid area of the college website. You can save time by searching for the external scholarships with your scholarship résumé. You may see national scholarship opportunities but save those until you have searched through the local scholarship opportunities.

Bonus Tip: If you have at least one semester before college graduation, take notes of future scholarships that fit you so you can save even more time when searching for scholarships for the next semester or year.

Government Websites (Local, City, State)

Be sure to check your government websites on all levels for scholarships that may be listed under your mayor's youth leadership program or educational programs for adult students, and scholarships that require students to complete the FAFSA on the state level. A quick way to search for government websites for scholarship opportunities is to use the search bar on the home page of the government website. Or, you can search in your favorite search engine using (name of local/city/state government) + scholarships.

Bonus Tip: Do you plan on attending college in another city or state? Research the local scholarship opportunities for current college students in that area.

Media (News Stations, Radio Stations, Newspapers, Magazines)

Local interest stories are huge for local media outlets because they know that people want to stay informed of what is happening in their town. Many scholarship organizations will send out a press release announcing that a scholarship opportunity is available as well as the scholarship winners. This is very important information to you for the following reasons:

1) You gain access to local scholarship opportunities.
2) News stories on the scholarship winners will provide insight into the scholarships that are available to you for future scholarship applications (and how to win them).

What does this mean for you? Watch your local news station, you're your local newspapers and magazines, and listen to your local radio stations weekly.

Bonus Tip: Be sure to search media outlets on the local, city, county, and state levels for scholarship opportunities. Since many media outlets have websites and social media accounts, you can get updates online or sign up for their newsletters, if available. Lastly, stay tuned for any college fairs or college expos that are scheduled to be in your area. They are usually free and provide scholarship information.

Charitable Organizations

Many scholarship providers are charitable organizations. As we discussed in the previous chapter, volunteer experience allows you to gain leadership experience, serve your community, and develop key skills to be successful in your future. These are qualities that scholarship judges want to see in your scholarship applications. Seek out local charities or local chapters of national and international charities for scholarship opportunities. Two great ways to find scholarships through charitable organizations are through direct involvement and by visiting local charitable organization websites or calling for scholarship opportunities.

Chamber of Commerce

Your local chamber of commerce is a community of local businesses and community leaders who can be a great source of scholarship opportunities to you. I encourage you to visit the chamber of commerce's website for upcoming community events, charity events for scholarship opportunities, and mentorship opportunities. Why? If you invest time in volunteering with the chamber of commerce or attending community events, you have the opportunity to develop relationships with the members. Through your relationship with them, you can gain an advantage when they announce their scholarship program. Also, they may share additional scholarship opportunities in the community with you. Lastly, don't hesitate to reach out to the chamber of commerce by phone or email for scholarship opportunities.

Career Services Center

This scholarship source is geared towards current college students (undergraduate and graduate students) but future college students can learn from this technique. Yes, you can and should approach the career services center on campus for scholarship opportunities. What's the connection between scholarships and careers? You are in college to learn skills that you will use in your chosen career field. You can lessen the burden of paying for college with scholarships so you can put more focus on developing your leadership skills and preparing for your future career. When you go to your career services center, you won't use the word scholarships when you ask for opportunities. Instead, ask the career services center staff if they know of any companies willing to pay for the remainder of your college education if you agree to work for the company upon graduation. Usually, this is known as co-operative (co-op) education program. If your college doesn't offer a co-op program for your degree program, use this technique.

College Alumni Association

The alumni association typically provides several scholarships for incoming and current college students. Depending on the process at your college, you may have to complete an additional scholarship application or will be automatically eligible when you get college acceptance. In terms of strategy, you have to find ways to build relationships with alumni members of your future or current college. The best way to build these relationships with alumni is to reach out to the local alumni chapter. These relationships can help strengthen your scholarship applications especially when applying for scholarships provided by the alumni association.

Future/Current College Students and College Graduates

Have you ever heard of the expression "two heads are better than one"? This is certainly the case when it comes to searching for scholarships. Even with your scholarship résumé, you may come across scholarships that don't fit you. This is not a problem because you can pass the scholarship information to another student who needs scholarships. Likewise, if you have access to college students who are in a higher class standing or college graduates, ask them about scholarship opportunities.

Bonus Tip: Parents, does your child lack the motivation to look for scholarships? Make the scholarship search a fun experience by hosting a scholarship search party for your child and his or her friends. Don't forget the snacks!

Employer (Human Resources Department)

Your employer may offer a tuition assistance program where they reimburse you for getting a college education related to your current position or scholarship program to pursue any college degree. Speak with your human resources manager about tuition reimbursement or scholarship opportunities yearly. Be sure to read the requirements carefully as you may be required to work for a certain amount of time or have to maintain a certain GPA to receive those benefits.

Special Note (Parents): If your child is headed to college, ask your human resources manager for scholarship opportunities.

Library

Even though most students search for scholarships with a range of digital devices, I want to encourage you to take advantage of the print resources available through the library. The general scholarship books are most beneficial when you go specifically to the areas of the books that apply to you based on your scholarship résumé. Also, ask your librarian for community and government resources for scholarship resources.

Bonus Tip: Take advantage of library resources to help you complete strong scholarship applications to increase your chances of winning scholarship dollars.

Contests

Contests are one of the most overlooked sources of scholarships. If you aren't finding enough traditional scholarships, I encourage you to apply for contests. I usually share this scholarship search strategy with K-6 students, but this strategy is open to all future and current college students. Like with traditional scholarships, start with contests that focus on a very specific theme from your scholarship résumé. For example, Google hosts the Doodle 4 Google contest every year for K-12 students to use creativity in designing their version of the Google logo. If you are artistic or desire to pursue a career in the arts, this is a great contest opportunity for you. I strongly advise you to save this scholarship source for last after you have completed your search for local, national, and international scholarships.

Bonus Tip: Keep track of the contests that you win so you can include them on your scholarship applications. Don't hesitate to mention your previously won contests on your other scholarship applications. I want to emphasize that these contests should be connected to your interests, talents, and achievements. This is a great way to set yourself apart from the other scholarship applicants.

Industry Associations

If you are interested in a specific industry or are wanting to further your education in your current career field, you can take advantage of local chapters representing industries that interest you.

1. Create a list of industry associations that interest you or are related to your current career field by using Weddle's Association Directory (http://www.weddles.com/associations). Or, you can use your favorite search engine to find industry associations (search for industry name + scholarship + city/state).

2. Visit the industry association websites for contact information for local industry chapters (city, state, or region) and scholarship opportunities. If you don't see scholarships listed on their website, visit their local office to ask about scholarship opportunities.

Bonus Tip: Use LinkedIn to find local industry associations, association members, and join online LinkedIn communities. I discuss this in detail in the social media section which is later in this chapter.

Bonus Tip: Are you looking for scholarships to complete a certification program? You are going to follow this same technique to find scholarships for your certification program.

Community Organizations

Community organizations are great scholarship resources because they have diverse programs that they fund to support members of the community including your college education. I strongly believe that a college education will be valuable to you for the rest of your life. And, community organizations agree with the value of education because they provide millions of dollars in scholarships and you can take advantage of this resource.

Bonus Tip: If you are a future college student that will be attending college out of town/state or current college student who has moved to another city to attend college, search for scholarships provided by communities where your college is located.

Bonus Tip: Don't neglect community organization websites with expired scholarship information! I discovered this scholarship source when I was working with a client who kept finding community organization websites with scholarship information from last year. Initially, I advised her to save the website link for next year. Several days later, I felt a strong need to email the community organization to attempt to get in contact with the director of the scholarship program. The director explained that the scholarship program was just renewed and that she would update the website at the end of the week. In the meantime, she emailed the scholarship application to me. The best part was that I was the first person to receive the scholarship application. I started working with my client on the scholarship application while the rest of the community wouldn't find out until the end of the week on the website. I want you to learn from this story that you must be thorough in your scholarship search and don't be afraid to follow up with the community organization if you see expired scholarship information.

Businesses

I want you to think about your local grocery store, banks, coffee shop, restaurants (local), laundromat, and clothing stores (local). I am sure you have made purchases at some of these businesses because they are a part of your community. The good news is that many businesses give back to their communities in the form of scholarships. Check with your school counselor or feel free to call their human resources departments for scholarship opportunities.

Bonus Tip: Don't forget to check bulletin boards in your local grocery stores and laundromats with local events, community highlights, fundraisers, and other information to help you find scholarships.

Bonus Tip: If a local business doesn't provide scholarships, ask if you can work for them in exchange for scholarship dollars. Speak with human resources and prepare a proposal

Social Media (Facebook, Twitter, Google Plus, Instagram, LinkedIn, and YouTube)

Social media is a great way to find scholarship opportunities. Why? Many organizations that provide scholarships have social media accounts. This is why you should be following these accounts and checking weekly for scholarships. While they may share promotions or services, they will share company news which includes scholarship opportunities. Also, don't neglect past scholarship announcements because you may learn key insights to help you win that particular scholarship from a social media post. Also, you can use social media platforms to create winning scholarship applications. I will discuss this in detail in Chapter 7. For now, I am going to cover each platform below with scholarship search strategies so that you don't waste time in the social media world.

Facebook: At the top of the Facebook website is a search bar that acts very similar to your favorite search engine. The only difference is that the search results will be specific to content on Facebook. I want you to take your search terms from your scholarship résumé plus your city or state and enter that information into the search bar. Also, you can search scholarships + city/state for scholarship opportunities. If you know the companies in your area, you can search by company name.

Bonus Tip: Don't forget about Facebook Pages and Groups! When you search with your search terms from your scholarship résumé in the search bar in Facebook, you will see additional tabs including Facebook Pages and Groups. Click on these tabs and like or join the Pages or Groups of organizations that provide scholarships or share scholarship resources. For example, if your future or current career field is culinary arts, you will search for culinary organizations. Make sure that the Facebook Group or Page is active with at least weekly updates.

Twitter: For the Twitter platform, hashtags (#) are your best friend along with search terms from your scholarship résumé. On the top right corner, you will see a search bar that says "Search Twitter". Enter your search terms from your scholarship résumé with and without hashtags so that you can capture all results. For example, if you are looking for scholarships for education majors, you may enter #education + #scholarships or education scholarships. Make sure to follow Twitter accounts of organizations that provide scholarships as well as organizations that provide lists of scholarships for all students.

Bonus Tip: Follow Twitter chats for scholarship resources. A Twitter chat is a 60-minute question and answer session where people gather to discuss a specific topic. I encourage you to search for a list of Twitter chats for college preparation, college admissions, scholarships, financial aid, and related to your future or current career field. Each Twitter chat will end each tweet with a hashtag so you can follow and participate in the conversation. Be sure to use the hashtag when you respond and ask questions. I invite you to join my weekly Twitter chat, #CollegeChat, and ask your scholarship questions.

Google Plus: Similar to the previous platforms, you will enter the search terms from your scholarship résumé into the search bar in Google Plus which is located in the top left side of the website. Be sure to search for communities (similar to Facebook Groups) that regularly share scholarship information. This platform is ideal for you if you desire to study abroad or desire to pursue a STEM (Science, Technology, Engineering, and Math) career. For example, if you are a current or future international student, you can enter "scholarships for international students" in the search bar and find communities as well as accounts of people who share international scholarship information. I advise you to join those communities and follow people who share scholarship information. If you are pursuing a STEM career field or currently work in a STEM career, you can search by your specific area (physics) to find scholarships just for your career field.

Instagram: Even though Instagram is mostly known for the fashion and business world, you will find that non-profit organizations, educators, school counselors, and industry associations share scholarship information using hashtags (#). The best ways to access scholarship resources on Instagram is to follow Instagram accounts and keep track of hashtags. Use your scholarship résumé and search for hashtags related to your search terms. For example, if you are searching for scholarships for the arts, media, or entertainment, you can search for #arts #scholarships or #media #scholarships or #entertainment #scholarships. Click on the magnifying glass in your Instagram account which is the second icon from the left side of your Instagram account.

LinkedIn: LinkedIn is similar to Facebook but is designed for professionals and industry organizations. This is good news for you so you can find scholarships offered by organizations in your community, industry organizations in your desired career field, and national scholarship organizations. Plus, you can get updates from LinkedIn industry groups in your desired career which may include early career exposure opportunities. LinkedIn can be complex, so I have created a simple plan for you below:

Step 1: **Set up your account with the right information.** When you set up your LinkedIn account, make sure to include information about your talents and achievements. If you gained volunteer or leadership experience with an organization, ask one of the organization members to share a recommendation of your experience on LinkedIn. They will need an account to share this information.

Step 2: **Join LinkedIn groups that provide scholarship opportunities.** Use your scholarship résumé and enter your search terms in the search bar in LinkedIn which is located at the top center of the website. For example, if your future or current career field is in government, you may search for government scholarships or scholarships for law majors. Make sure to add LinkedIn groups for your city or state.

Step 3: **Follow companies that provide scholarship opportunities.** From searching for scholarships using your favorite search engine, I am sure you noticed the websites of companies providing scholarships. I want you to take the names of those companies, search for them using the search bar in LinkedIn, and follow them. When you follow companies on LinkedIn, you will get all of their latest updates including scholarship information.

YouTube: As I mentioned in the beginning of this section, organizations that provide scholarship opportunities have social media accounts including YouTube. Additionally, colleges and universities along with those who work in education provide scholarship sources and strategies to help you find more money for college. The best way to find these organizations and scholarship tips is to use your search terms from your scholarship résumé. For example, if your future or current career field is psychology, you will search for scholarships for psychology majors. Don't forget to make note of videos of past scholarship winners for scholarships that fit you. This will give you information on what you should include in your future scholarship applications.

Places of Worship

Yes, your local places of worship may have a scholarship opportunity for you. Take time to speak with your youth director for scholarship opportunities. If your place of worship doesn't currently have a scholarship program, create a proposal and present it to the leadership team to start a scholarship program. The scholarship program can be funded through fundraisers or donations if the budget isn't available to provide students with scholarships.

Bonus Tip: Seek out scholarships associated with your denomination. For example, if you are a member of the Methodist denomination, you can contact the local, regional, and international offices for scholarship opportunities.

Google Alerts

Are you interested in getting scholarship opportunities emailed to you for free? I know you are busy and this is a great and easy strategy to help you stay informed of upcoming scholarships. Follow the simple steps below:

1. Visit www.google.com/alerts.

2. Enter your search terms from your scholarship résumé into the "Create an alert about" box.

3. Click on Show Options to determine how often you want to receive scholarship opportunities and what type of search results you want to receive, and other features.

4. Click Create Alert.

Now, you are ready to start receiving scholarship opportunities to your inbox. If you are a future or current college student, I highly advise you set up Google Alerts now.

Apps

Did you know that there are apps that you can use to search for scholarships? To make sure that you aren't leaving any scholarship dollars, you can search in your favorite search engine for apps + (insert search term from your scholarship résumé) + local/city/state. I advise you to download the free scholarship search apps before paying for scholarship search apps. You may decide that you don't wish to pay for an app. You aren't required to pay for a scholarship search app to find scholarships.

Take action!

Select a minimum of three sources of scholarships to get started. After you have researched those opportunities, select another set of scholarship sources that I have discussed above. Get started today!

CHAPTER 5

NATIONAL AND INTERNATIONAL
SCHOLARSHIP SEARCH STRATEGIES

"Don't neglect national and international scholarship opportunities that fit you because you don't want to leave any scholarship dollars on the table". – Ashley Hill

Introduction

Yes, the competition with national and international scholarship opportunities is greater than local scholarship opportunities, but you now know what will make your scholarship applications rise above the competition. The competition is no longer a factor when you focus on making sure that your scholarship applications represent you will and highlights your leadership skills. I have seen students focus on thinking about who else is applying for the scholarship and if they have a real chance of winning the scholarship. This shouldn't be your mindset with applying for scholarships especially on the national and international levels. When you follow the steps in the book, you will recognize which scholarships fit you and you will only focus on applying for them.

Please note that national scholarship opportunities are referring to scholarships outside of your local area, city, county, and state.

Now, I am going to discuss national and international sources of scholarships along with the strategies that you can use to get started finding the national and international scholarships that fit you today. The best approach to finding and winning scholarships is to search with your scholarship résumé. For example, if you are an athlete applying for a national athletic scholarship, you certainly qualify but many other athletes will qualify as well. What separates you from all of the other athletes? Your leadership skills! You have to be able to show the judges your strengths and abilities beyond the basic requirement of being an athlete.

Let's get started.

National Scholarship Sources and Strategies

Since the national scholarship search strategies will be very similar to how you will search for local scholarships, I am going to list the scholarship sources followed by the summary of national scholarship search strategies.

National Scholarship Sources
The following scholarship resources are great sources of national scholarship opportunities:

Your Favorite Search Engine
College Financial Aid/College Admissions Websites
Scholarship Search Websites
Government Websites
Industry Organizations
Associations
Memberships
School Counselor (K-12 Students)
Social Media
Google Alerts
PSAT
Charitable Organizations
Apps
College Preparation/Admissions/Scholarships Websites
Library
Bookstores

National Scholarship Search Strategies

As you look at the list of scholarship sources above, I want you to understand that the major difference in how you find local scholarships and national scholarships is the search terms you use from your scholarship résumé. With local scholarships, it is very easy to narrow down scholarships by location because everyone living outside of that area is automatically not eligible for the scholarship. When you start searching for scholarships on the national level, the number of students applying for those scholarships is much higher than on the local level. This presents a challenge but I can tell you that you are up for the challenge because you have a unique set of life experiences. It will be difficult to win a scholarship when you mention that you have a 3.0 GPA and everyone else has the same GPA. What everyone else doesn't have is your life experiences. Focus on your unique qualities, leadership experience, talents, and achievements throughout your scholarship applications to give you a higher chance of winning scholarship dollars.

The key is to concentrate on national scholarships with a narrow focus. In fact, this is where scholarship search websites can be very valuable to you. You can follow this same principle when searching in the large scholarship books in your local library or bookstore.

Bonus Tip: Do you want to study abroad? There are scholarships to assist you in paying for your semester or year studying abroad. Start with your financial aid or international student office which is a great source of scholarship opportunities. Next, research US government-sponsored scholarship programs such as the Critical Language Scholarship program. Lastly, search for other search terms in your favorite search engine such as cultural exchange or study in (foreign city or country). The key is to start early!

Bonus Tip: When you are searching for national scholarships online, don't include "national" with your search terms. You will get back search results with scholarships that don't fit you because every website with national scholarship will be included in those search results. The only time you should include national with your search terms is when you are searching for national associations.

Bonus Tip: Do you desire to send your child to private K-12 school but need scholarships? There are scholarship programs for private K-12 students but you have to read the requirements very carefully to ensure that your child is indeed eligible for those scholarship dollars. Two great resources are the Young Scholar's Program which is directed by the Jack Kent Cooke Foundation and the A Better Chance Referral Program.

International Scholarship Sources and Strategies

Now, I want to transition to discussing international scholarship sources and strategies. If you live outside of the United States of America and desire to pursue your college education outside of your resident country, these sources and scholarship strategies are for you.

Let's get started.

First, the most important thing that I want you to learn in this chapter is that there are international scholarships. There tends to be more requirements with international scholarship opportunities, so you have to make sure that you are 100% eligible for the scholarships. You don't want your scholarship application to be rejected because of failure to meet all of the requirements. Next, I highly advise you to start searching for scholarships at least 18 months before you plan to attend college or university. Please start as early as possible. I am going to discuss each scholarship source and the strategies you can use to find your scholarships today.

Websites for International Students

A great way to find the scholarships that fit you is to focus on websites created for international students, so I recommend that you get started by visiting the following websites:

InternationalScholarships.com
IEFA.org (International Education Financial Aid)
InternationalStudent.com
Scholars4Dev.com (Scholarships for Development)

You will get the most benefit out of these websites if you have a list of potential colleges that you would like to attend as well as potential degree programs.

College Financial/Admissions Websites

When you have selected a college where you wish to study, be sure to take time to visit the admissions and financial aid areas of the college's websites for funding for international students. Colleges with large populations of international students may have an office dedicated to helping you apply for college as well as find scholarships. If this office exists at your desired college, take advantage and call or email with your questions.

Bonus Tip: Contact the department of your desired degree program for possible scholarships to help you pay for your college education.

Government-Sponsored Scholarship Programs

Yes, some scholarship programs for international students are sponsored by the United States of America government such as the Fulbright Foreign Student Program. I encourage you to search for similar programs on the international student websites as well as ask the college admissions staff at your desired college or university. Also, research government-sponsored scholarship programs in your home country such as the scholarships for Indian students pursuing research careers in science and technology under the Agency for Science, Technology, and Research which was sponsored by the Indian government and Singapore.

Foundations

Research foundations in your area and country for possible scholarships. For example, the Inlaks Foundation provides scholarships to Indian citizens residing in India to attend college or university in the United States of America, the United Kingdom, and other European countries.

International Student College Admissions Fairs

Organizations such as the Institute of International Education will host fairs in Asia and India to give international students a chance to speak with US college admissions representatives. This is a great opportunity to ask your questions about applying for scholarships and other funding opportunities to help you pay for your college. Contact your potential colleges you wish to attend abroad and ask if they host events in your area.

Social Media (Google Plus, Twitter, LinkedIn, Facebook)

You will find thousands of international student scholarship resources across the Google Plus, Twitter, LinkedIn, and Facebook platforms. In fact, I encourage you to create your accounts on those social media websites today! Please refer to the "Social Media" section in the previous chapter for how to find scholarships in a just a few simple steps. The greatest way to take advantage of these social media websites is to connect with the organizations that provide international student scholarships. Lastly, join international student groups on these social media websites so you can get all of the updates on upcoming scholarships that fit you.

Take action!

Please select three scholarship sources from the list above and research those sources for scholarships for you today. Remember, start as early as possible.

CHAPTER 6

WRITING STRONG SCHOLARSHIP ESSAYS

"Your scholarship essay is your time to shine and communicate the best representation of yourself to the scholarship judges". – Ashley Hill

Introduction

I know that you may not be fond of writing scholarship essays, but I want to share with you why many scholarship requirements include scholarship essays. Scholarship judges don't have background information on your life and your experiences. They will develop a perspective of you based on your scholarship application including your scholarship essay. Writing a scholarship essay requires you to articulate and communicate your thoughts effectively to the scholarship judges. Scholarship judges aren't handing out scholarship dollars to everyone. You will have to put forth effort (just like you will put forth effort in your college courses).

Special Note: I am seeing too many students searching for easy scholarships, scholarships without essay requirements, or contests where they just enter name and email. Please avoid searching for these type of scholarships. You will have better success with winning scholarship dollars when you pursue scholarships that require you to write scholarship essays or answer short questions.

What are scholarship judges wanting to see in the scholarship essay?

Scholarship judges want to see that you have followed the directions such as with word count and answering the scholarship essay question completely. Most of all, scholarship judges want to see evidence of your leadership experiences. Why? Organizations that provide scholarships are interested in supporting students who will impact the world with their college education. What type of people impact the world? Leaders!

Special Note: Any leadership experiences that you include in your scholarship essay need to be meaningful experiences. Meaningful leadership experiences focus on your service to others. Scholarship judges don't want to read about how you need a scholarship to be a physician to buy a large home and luxury car.

Writing Strong Scholarship Essays

Now, I am going to share with you the elements of strong scholarship essays. The best way to strengthen your scholarship essay writing skills is through practice. Start as early as possible so you can have enough time to edit the scholarship essay and send it to the scholarship committee before the deadline. Please keep in mind that you must meet all requirements of the scholarship essay. These requirements include the following:

Answer the scholarship essay question or prompt. This is not the time to get creative and write a scholarship essay with a lot of moving parts. Write a clear and concise scholarship essay.

Word count. Do not write over the limit. This shows the scholarship judges that you don't follow directions or failed to read the directions.

Bonus Tip: Make your scholarship essay come alive by using active verbs such as gained, identified, and created. Make sure to follow all grammar and spelling rules.

Bonus Tip: Make sure to add your name and page number in the top right corner of each page of your scholarship résumé. As the scholarship judges review your scholarship essay, your pages may get separated. You don't want to make the scholarship judges work harder than necessary to put your scholarship essay pages back together.

What is the first task you must complete when writing your scholarship essay?

The first thing you need to do is visit the organization's website and read the mission and purpose. Why? The organization reveals through its reason for existing and who it serves through its mission and purpose. In other words, the organization is sharing what is a priority to them. For example, if the organization's mission is to end poverty and its purpose is to provide food for impoverished children, you have just learned what matters most to the organization. This organization seeks to make an impact in the lives of children who don't have access to enough food to sustain them. This is leadership in action. So, your scholarship essay should discuss examples when you actively led an initiative or project. Ideally, if you worked with youth or have a passion for working with children, this would be a great addition to the essay in this example. You don't want to just state that you are a leader. You have to give examples of your leadership experience because you must remember that the judges don't have the insight or background knowledge of your leadership skills. This is also known as the "show and not tell" concept. Ultimately, you want to make a connection between your leadership experience through your unique qualities (life experiences) and the mission and purpose of the organization providing the scholarship.

How do I discuss sensitive topics such as personal or health challenges?

First, you have the power to decide if you even want to share personal information. Please understand that if you decide to share sensitive information in your scholarship essay (or scholarship application), your essay may be published on the organization's website. Secondly, I advise you to share personal challenges in general manner, but highlight how you have overcome that challenge. You have to be careful not to put too much emphasis on the challenge because that would cause scholarship judges to possibly feel like you are just focused on you and your struggles. For example, if you have juvenile diabetes, you can mention your experience with disease and how you are impacting the lives of others by volunteering with health organizations to educate people on diabetes prevention. Or, if you were assaulted, you can discuss how you used that painful moment in your life to encourage and serve others in your community. You should always discuss the challenge with how you are using that experience to further develop as a leader (making a positive impact on others). Lastly, you don't have to give every detail of your challenge. You should take no more than two to three sentences to describe your challenge. Keep the emphasis on the essay prompt and displaying your leadership experience through your life experiences.

What's the formula for writing a strong scholarship essay?

Truly, there is no formula for writing strong scholarship essays. Some students believe in writing three paragraphs for beginning, middle, and end. Others may believe in writing five paragraphs for introduction, three paragraphs with supporting details, and a conclusion. These are just two examples, but every student is different. You have to find a strategy that works for your writing style.

I suggest that you begin with an opening statement that will get the attention of the scholarship judges. Please do not begin your scholarship essay with a quote or simply stating the prompt. Instead, I suggest that you begin with a story over two three sentences. Don't tell the entire story in those few sentences but leave the scholarship judges in suspense.

Next, connect your opening story to the essay prompt. I advise you to be very concise and write clear and simple sentences. If the scholarship judge is unable to make the connection between your opening story and the scholarship essay prompt, your chances of winning that scholarship are in jeopardy. Also, be sure to include your leadership experience through your life experiences in this middle section. Give clear examples and use active verbs to show the scholarship judges how you are a leader in the examples. Lastly, make sure that each sentence flows with the theme of the scholarship essay.

In your final section of your scholarship essay, you want to summarize your points without repeating the exact words in the earlier sections of your essay. Put emphasis on your leadership experience, lessons that you learned from those experiences, and make the connection to the scholarship essay prompt.

Bonus Tip: Don't end your scholarship essay with asking for scholarship money or hinting that you deserve the scholarship. The scholarship judges will quickly move that essay and your scholarship application to the discard pile.

Bonus Tip: Are you working and attending college? Don't hesitate to mention in your scholarship essay that winning this scholarship will allow you to focus completely on your college program.

How can my scholarship strategy team help me write strong scholarship essays?

Your scholarship resource team can assist you with brainstorming how you can incorporate your leadership experiences through your life experience. Also, a member of your scholarship resource team may have insight into the organization providing the scholarship that you should include in your scholarship essay. One of the best ways that your scholarship strategy team can assist you in writing strong scholarship essays is to help you clarify your thoughts and provide feedback or corrections. Sometimes, it is difficult to miss grammatical or spelling errors with your own work. Ask one or two members of your scholarship strategy team to review your scholarship essay before sending it to the scholarship committee.

Take Action!

There is no better time than right now to get started writing your scholarship essays. I want you to select one scholarship application that requires you to write a scholarship essay. Create a goal to write your first draft of the scholarship essay in the next seven days. Meet with one or two members of your scholarship strategy team to get feedback. Make your necessary revisions and send it the scholarship committee.

CHAPTER 7

CREATE WINNING SCHOLARSHIP APPLICATIONS

"You create winning scholarship applications by focusing on the one thing that makes your scholarship application stand out – your unique qualities". – Ashley Hill

Introduction

I want you to think of each scholarship application like a puzzle. You have the pieces which include the scholarship requirements, scholarship essay, your leadership experience, and your unique qualities. Now, you just have to put the pieces of the puzzle together. Your scholarship application communicated who you are to the scholarship judges. The first impression that the scholarship judges have of you is the lasting impression. You want to make sure that the scholarship judges see the best representation of you which is also known as your brand.

Since I have discussed all of the pieces to the puzzle (scholarship application) in previous chapters, I am going to show you how to put those pieces together in this chapter. Before I start, please make sure that you have your scholarship résumé. You will need to add relevant information to your scholarship application.

Now, do you remember the number one thing that I mentioned that scholarship judges want to see on your scholarship applications? Scholarship judges want to see evidence of your leadership experience. You show your leadership experience through your experiences, talents, and achievements. Leadership experience with your unique qualities has to remain the focus of the scholarship application.

How to Show Leadership, Talents, and Achievements on Your Scholarship Applications

You will approach your scholarship applications in the same way that you approach your scholarship essay. You want to make sure that the information that you include from your scholarship résumé is relevant to the organization's mission and purpose for offering the scholarship opportunity. For this reason, you will not include every activity or every leadership experience on your scholarship application. Focus on putting the pieces of the puzzle together that fits based on the theme of the scholarship opportunity. Some organizations ask to see a list of your activities. I encourage you to include the academic, volunteer, and internship sections of your scholarship résumé if the organization requests to see a list of your activities. Most importantly, be authentic. You don't have to use large words or try to imitate anyone else. When you focus on your unique qualities in meeting the scholarship requirements, you give yourself the best chance of winning the scholarship.

Recommendation Letters 101

One of the most common mistakes that students make with recommendation letters is asking for them too late. You should ask for recommendation letters as soon as you decide to apply for a scholarship. You don't want the person writing the recommendation letter to rush and leave out important details to meet a short deadline. Next, ask him or her for a strong letter of recommendation and provide your scholarship resume. This allows the person to highlight examples of your character and your activities. Also, don't be afraid to follow up with the person writing your letter of recommendation if you are two to three weeks from your scholarship application deadline. After the person has written a strong letter of recommendation for you, don't forget to give them a handwritten note to thank them for their contribution to helping you find and win scholarships.

What should I do after I send my scholarship application to the scholarship judges?

After you send the scholarship application to the scholarship judges, send a short email thanking them for the opportunity (local scholarships only) or connect with them on social media thanking them for the opportunity (national and international scholarships). This makes you memorable with the scholarship committee and will help strengthen your chances of winning scholarship dollars.

What should I do after I win a scholarship?

Congratulations! Make sure to send a handwritten note thanking the committee for selecting you as the scholarship winner within one week of winning the scholarship. Handwritten notes provide a personal touch with the scholarship committee. I can tell you that many students skip this crucial step which could lead to further opportunities in the future.

Bonus Tip: Please pay attention to scholarship eligibility requirements. If your scholarship requires you to have a specific grade point average or join an association, or attend meetings, be sure to follow the rules. Failure to follow the requirements could cause you to become ineligible and lose the scholarship funds.

Take action!

As you begin to work on your scholarship applications, review them to see if you are focus on displaying your leadership experience through your life experiences.

CHAPTER 8

FINAL THOUGHTS: GET MORE MONEY FOR COLLEGE NOW!

"You already qualify for merit scholarships based on your talents and achievements. It's time that you create strong applications that get the attention of the scholarship judges". —
Ashley Hill

Introduction

Scholarship Search and Application Process

Let's review the process that I have discussed in the previous chapters.

1. Create your goal for the scholarship amount you estimate that you will need to cover the costs of your college educations.
2. Develop the right mindset by understanding the three core beliefs in the world of scholarships.
3. Create your scholarship résumé.
4. Review each section of your scholarship résumé and add synonyms to help you find scholarships that fit you in less time.
5. Create your scholarship strategy based on your scholarship résumé.
6. Build your scholarship strategy team.
7. Use local scholarship sources and search strategies to find and win scholarships that fit you in your area.
8. Use national and international sources and search strategies to find and win scholarships that fit you.
9. Write strong scholarship essays that highlight your leadership experience through your life experiences.
10. Create winning scholarship applications by focusing on your unique qualities and leadership experience.

Do you want even more scholarship search and application resources?

I have created the Ultimate Scholarship Tool Kit for Finding and Winning More Money for College Now to say thank you for investing in yourself by reading the scholarship search and application strategies in this guide. To receive your free Ultimate Scholarship Tool Kit for Finding and Winning More Money for College Now, please send an email to collegeprepready@gmail.com with proof that you purchased this guide.

The additional resources include a list of corporations that provide scholarships, recommendation letter templates, financial aid appeal letter templates, scholarship websites, and more.

Take action!

I want you to read the review of the process to find and win scholarships that fit you now very carefully. Make sure that you understand how each section helps you to find and win scholarships. Now, you have all of the knowledge and strategies that you need to search for scholarships that fit you and win them.

I challenge you to take the next seven days to search for scholarships and complete at least one scholarship application. Remember that you already qualify for merit scholarships. Apply the knowledge that I have shared in this guide to find and win those scholarships that fit you now!

ABOUT THE AUTHOR

Ashley Hill is the CEO and Founder of ALH Group LLC which manages the College Prep Ready program. She is a Scholarship Search Strategist who teaches overwhelmed and stressed students (elementary – doctoral students) and their families around the world how to lower the cost of college with a simple step-by-step solution that leverages their talents and achievements to maximize their potential to win merit scholarships. She is a speaker, workshop facilitator, and conference host of the annual College Success Conference. Ashley earned a Bachelor of Arts degree in Biology from Kent State University in 2008. Additionally, she earned a Master of Public Health degree with a concentration in Public Policy from A. T. Still University in 2011.